REPTILES & AMPHIBIANS
Coloring Book

THOMAS C. QUIRK, Jr.

Text by Professor Samuel Gundy
Kutztown State College

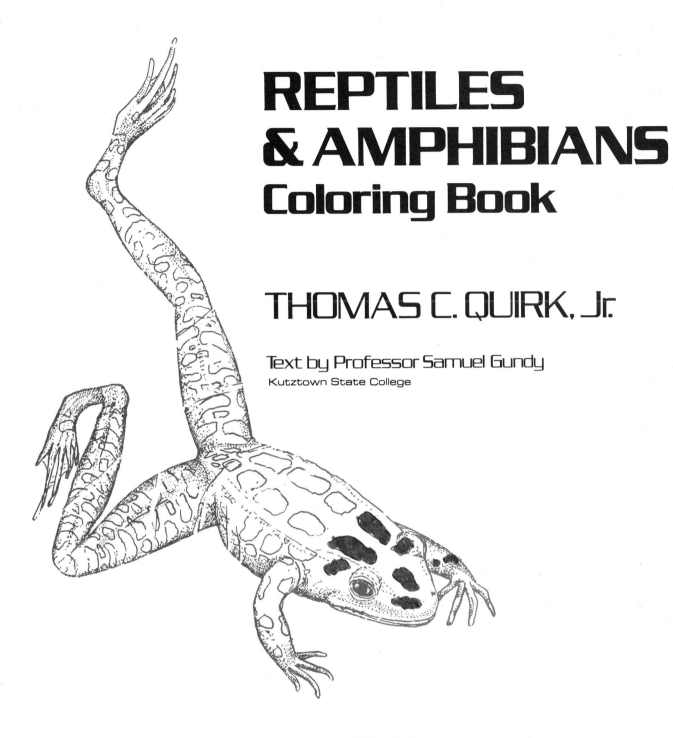

Dover Publications, Inc.
New York

PUBLISHER'S NOTE

Reptiles and amphibians are vertebrates, as are fish, birds, and mammals (the group that human beings belong to). Zoologists distinguish reptiles by the following traits: they breathe with lungs; their body temperature varies (this feature is commonly known as being cold-blooded); they have a skin with scales; and their eggs are fertilized internally. Amphibians too are cold-blooded, but they have skin without scales, and to a great degree they respire through it. Most amphibians lay their eggs in the water; the larvae have gills and live in the water, but later they metamorphose or change into adults without gills. Scientists can easily tell present-day reptiles apart from present-day amphibians merely by comparing their skeletons, but the ancestors of reptiles were very similar to the ancestors of amphibians, and it is hard to distinguish between the two groups on the basis of their fossil remains.

The various classes of amphibians and reptiles can be broken down further into increasingly smaller categories until we get to an individual species, which is a group of animals capable of breeding together. Making these distinctions is not always difficult; all of us can tell an American Alligator from a Water Moccasin, even though both are reptiles, and we can be sure those animals know the difference too, especially during mating season. Sometimes, however, even zoologists can't agree on where to draw the line between species, but classifying living things is important because it shows us the evolutionary relationships among animals and gives us clues as to the way a particular species has adapted to the environment.

For this reason the captions accompanying the pictures presented here for coloring provide the animals' scientific as well as their common names.

The forty-five illustrations in the *Reptiles and Amphibians Coloring Book*, often with several animals per picture, will provide you with a delightful coloring experience. The captions will guide you with suggestions regarding animals' actual coloration. All of the pictures are reproduced with authentic coloration on the covers as well. Similar animals have been put into groups—crocodiles, snakes, lizards, and turtles are reptiles; salamanders and frogs are amphibians. The artist has carefully placed each animal in its natural habitat so that you can see how and where it lives. The captions will also tell you how large the real reptiles and amphibians are, where they can be found, what they eat, what eats them, how they behave, and how they have adapted to their environment. Did you know that the cold-blooded alligator basks in the sun in order to keep its blood at the right temperature? (And you thought it was just lazy!) Did you know that the fantastic lizard known as the Green Basilisk gets its name from a legendary beast said to kill people simply by looking at them? Did you know that the best turtle for turtle soup is not, strictly speaking, a turtle at all but a terrapin? Besides the pleasure of coloring the pictures, this book will provide you with an introduction to the curious, sometimes humorous, often eerie world of reptiles and amphibians.

Copyright © 1981 by Dover Publications, Inc.
All rights reserved under Pan American and International Copyright Conventions.

Published in Canada by General Publishing Company, Ltd., 30 Lesmill Road, Don Mills, Toronto, Ontario.

Published in the United Kingdom by Constable and Company, Ltd., 3 The Lanchesters, 162–164 Fulham Palace Road, London W6 9ER.

Reptiles and Amphibians Coloring Book is a new work, first published by Dover Publications, Inc., in 1981.

DOVER *Pictorial Archive* SERIES

This book belongs to the Dover Pictorial Archive Series. You may use the designs and illustrations for graphics and crafts applications, free and without special permission, provided that you include no more than four in the same publication or project. (For permission for additional use, please write to Dover Publications, Inc., 31 East 2nd Street, Mineola, N.Y. 11501.)

However, republication or reproduction of any illustration by any other graphic service whether it be in a book or in any other design resource is strictly prohibited.

International Standard Book Number: 0-486-24111-4

Manufactured in the United States of America
Dover Publications, Inc.
31 East 2nd Street
Mineola, N.Y. 11501

AMERICAN ALLIGATOR *[Alligator mississippiensis].* Although its range has been tremendously reduced by land drainage and the fashion for alligator bags, shoes, and belts, this alligator is still found from the Carolinas to eastern Texas in rivers, canals, lakes, bayous, and marshes. It basks along the riverbank and rests in the water with only its head, sometimes only eyes and nostrils, showing. Blackish colored, it is shown here capturing a **WATER MOCCASIN** or **COTTON-MOUTH SNAKE** *[Agkistrodon piscivorus],* a venomous water snake that may grow to four feet in length, found from North Carolina to Alabama and as far north as southern Illinois. It has a dark line through the eye and along the side of its head, dark crossbands, and a ground color ranging from olive to black. The inside of its mouth is cotton white.

1

INDIAN GAVIAL *[Gavialis gangeticus]* (TOP). Frequently called **GHARIAL** after a clay jar *(gharal)* found in India shaped like its head, this reptile has a very long, narrow snout with more teeth than any other crocodile. Its nostrils and eyes are set high up, permitting the Gavial, which reaches 20 feet in length, to see and breathe while keeping the rest of its body underwater. It is found in rivers of north India. The once-widespread **AMERICAN CROCODILE** *[Crocodylus acutus]* (BOTTOM) now has breeding populations only in the Everglades National Park and the Florida Keys. Reaching 16 feet in length, adults are gray with a tapering snout and a prominent fourth tooth in the lower jaw. They prefer fresh water but may be found in salt or brackish waters.

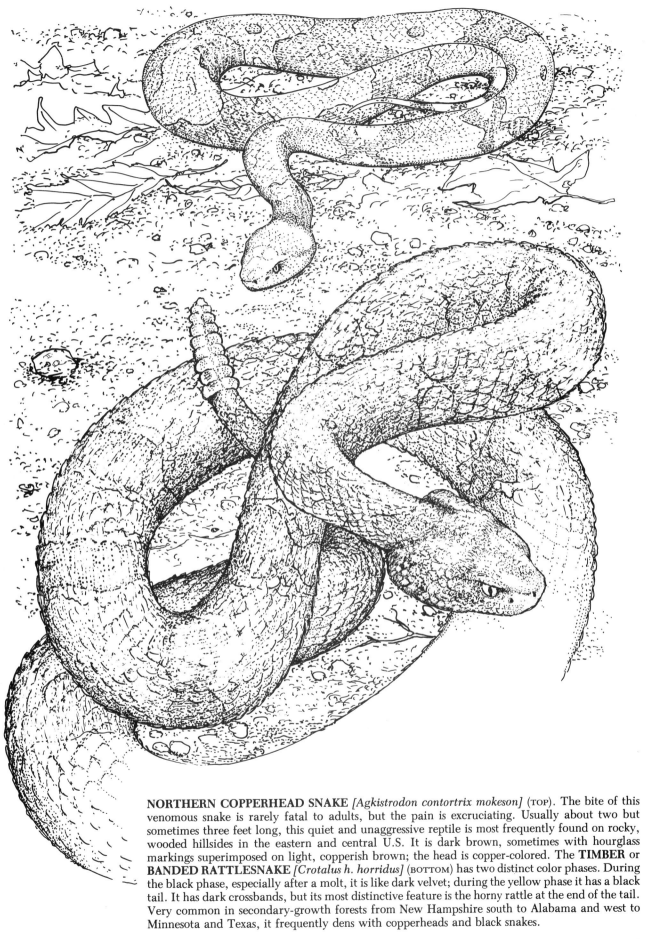

NORTHERN COPPERHEAD SNAKE *[Agkistrodon contortrix mokeson]* (TOP). The bite of this venomous snake is rarely fatal to adults, but the pain is excruciating. Usually about two but sometimes three feet long, this quiet and unaggressive reptile is most frequently found on rocky, wooded hillsides in the eastern and central U.S. It is dark brown, sometimes with hourglass markings superimposed on light, copperish brown; the head is copper-colored. The **TIMBER** or **BANDED RATTLESNAKE** *[Crotalus h. horridus]* (BOTTOM) has two distinct color phases. During the black phase, especially after a molt, it is like dark velvet; during the yellow phase it has a black tail. It has dark crossbands, but its most distinctive feature is the horny rattle at the end of the tail. Very common in secondary-growth forests from New Hampshire south to Alabama and west to Minnesota and Texas, it frequently dens with copperheads and black snakes.

SCARLET KING SNAKE *[Lampropeltis triangulum elap-soides]* (TOP). An attractively colored, harmless snake with smooth scales, it is often confused with the venomous **COR-AL SNAKE** *(Micrurus f. fulvius)* (not pictured). The major difference is that the Scarlet's head is red, the Coral's black. A nocturnal species about 20 inches long, it hides beneath logs and woodland debris in a range extending from North Carolina south to Florida and west to the Mississippi River. The **RED MILK SNAKE** *[Lampropeltis triangulum syspila]* (BOT-TOM) is a showy snake with red blotches on a whitish ground. Its belly scutes are prominently checkered black and white. Over two feet long, it is a good "mouser" and is found in rocky, wooded hills in the central U.S.

There are 75 varieties of water or grass snakes, most of them found in the Old World, a few in North America. The **RED-BANDED WATER SNAKE** *[Natrix f. fasciata]* (OPPOSITE, TOP) is characterized by crossbands that run the entire length of its body and a dark eye-stripe set at an angle to the jaw. This snake's color may vary from reddish to yellow or brown. It is found on the coastal plain from North Carolina to Louisiana, excluding Florida. The **MIDLAND** or **MIDWEST WA-TER SNAKE** *[Natrix sipedon pleuralis]* (OPPOSITE, MIDDLE) may reach 3½ feet in length. There is considerable color varia-tion; its dark bands are smaller than the spaces between them, a characteristic that helps to distinguish it from the **NORTH-ERN WATER SNAKE** *(Natrix s. sipedon)* (not pictured). The Midland Snake is commonly found in streams, ponds, and marshes in the Midwest. The four-foot **BLOTCHED WATER SNAKE** *[Natrix erythrogaster transversa]* (OPPOSITE, BOTTOM) is, as the name *erythrogaster* implies, closely related to the **RED-BELLIED SNAKE** *[Storeria occipitomaculata]* (not pictured). It has widely varied coloration, and is found along rivers and ditches in the south-central U.S.

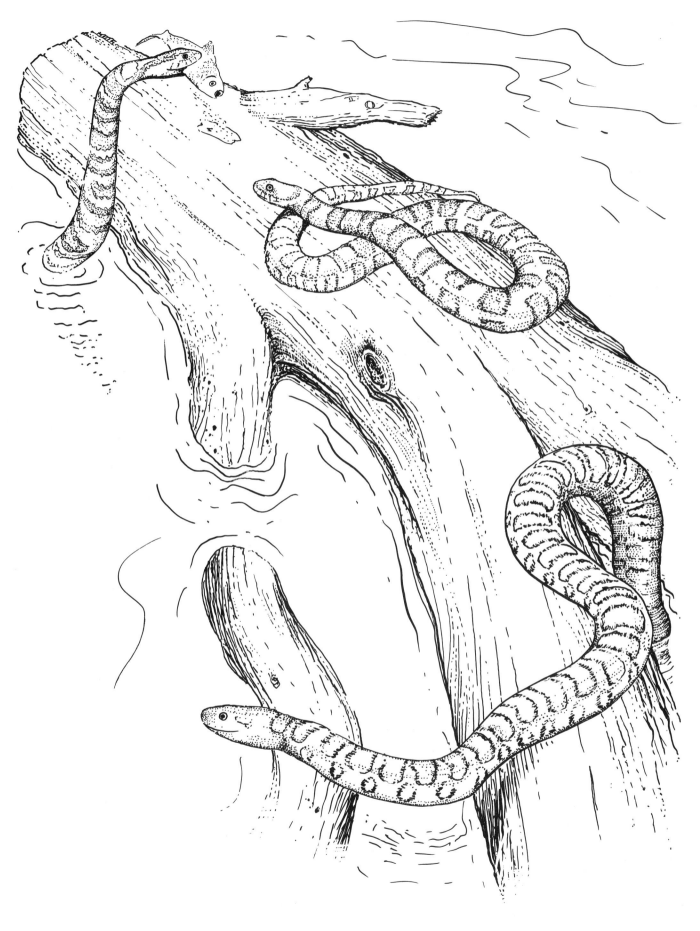

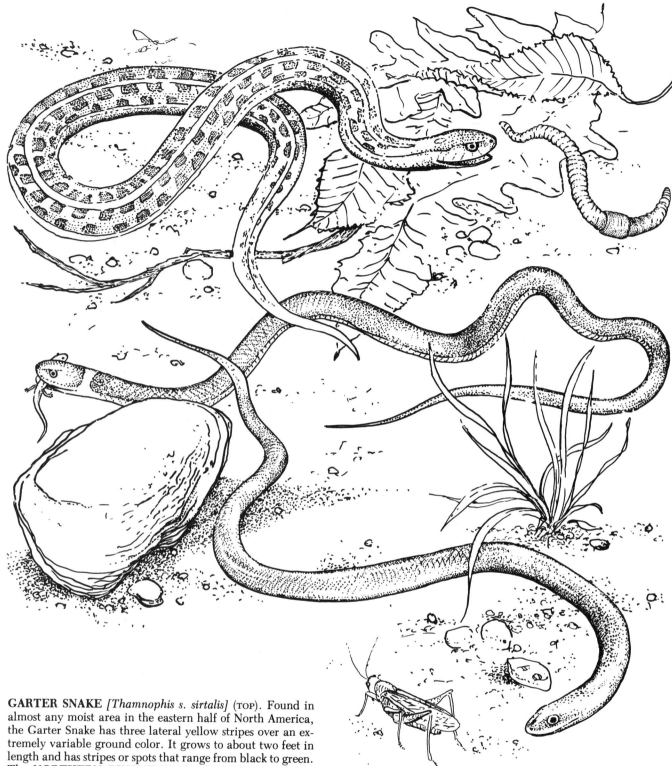

GARTER SNAKE *[Thamnophis s. sirtalis]* (TOP). Found in almost any moist area in the eastern half of North America, the Garter Snake has three lateral yellow stripes over an extremely variable ground color. It grows to about two feet in length and has stripes or spots that range from black to green. The **NORTHERN RINGNECK SNAKE** *[Diadophis punctatus edwardsi]* (MIDDLE) is about one foot long and colored black except for a yellow ring around the neck. It is found under logs and stones from Nova Scotia south to Georgia and west to Wisconsin. There are no markings on the **SMOOTH GREEN SNAKE** *[Opheodrys vernalis]* (BOTTOM), which may exceed 1½ feet in length. Sometimes found in "quaking" bogs (that is, bodies of water that become overgrown with moss, plants, and even trees and that "quake" when you walk on them) but more often in grassy meadows, it may be an upland or lowland snake, depending on what part of its range —southeastern Canada to northeastern U.S.— it lives in.

YELLOW RAT SNAKE *[Elaphe obsoleta quadrivittata]* (OPPOSITE). This bright-golden constrictor of the southeastern U.S. becomes less colorful as it reaches its northernmost distribution toward North Carolina. Habitats include woodlands, marshes, scrub country, and coastal areas. It suffocates its prey, like the rat in our picture, by wrapping its six-foot-long body around it. Once dead, the prey is swallowed at leisure. This species is also called the **YELLOW CHICKEN SNAKE**, because of an alternative food, and the **STRIPED HOUSE SNAKE**, because of its four dark stripes.

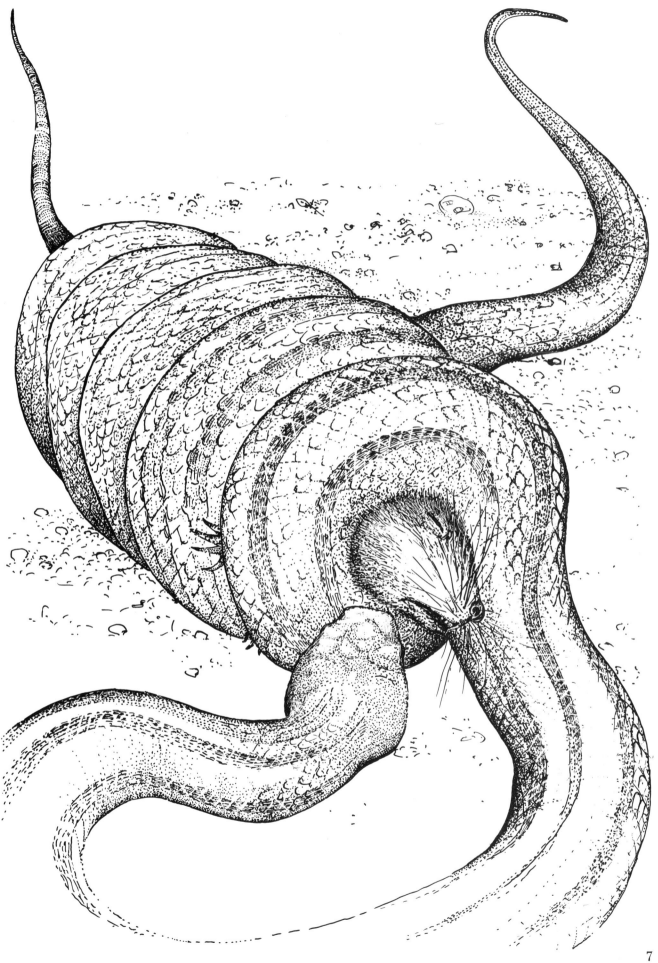

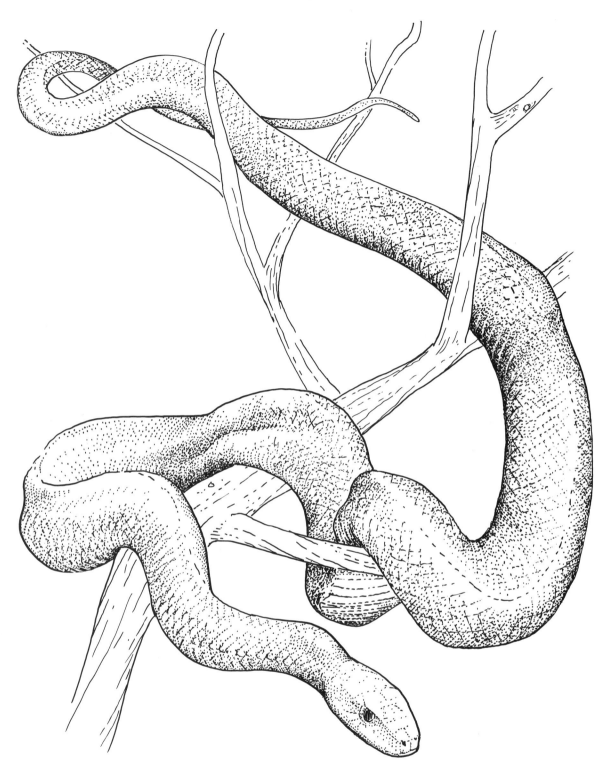

EASTERN GREEN MAMBA *[Dendroaspis angusticeps].*
There are three species of green mambas and one of black in
Africa. The **BLACK MAMBA** *[Dendroaspis polylepsis]* (not
pictured), an especially dangerous terrestrial snake, is green-
ish when young; all the exclusively green species are arboreal
with highly toxic venom. All mambas are large, slender, and
very fast, and have two large tubular fangs toward the front
of the mouth. The highly alert but unaggressive Eastern
Green Mamba, found in forests and brush country in eastern
Africa, grows to eight feet and is often confused with the extremely dangerous **BOOMSLANG** *[Dispholidus typus]* (not
pictured).

GABOON VIPER *[Bitis gabonica]* (OPPOSITE). The beautiful
and often brilliantly colored Gaboon Viper features blues and
tans, mixed with black and some white, in a broken pattern
that makes it difficult to discern among the leaves and litter of
the forest floor. A large, thick-bodied snake that may grow to
six feet, it has a tan head with a pair of triangular "horns" between the nostrils and fangs up to two inches long that deliver
the hemotoxic venom (that is, poison that attacks the blood)
characteristic of the vipers. Although its bite is usually lethal,
fortunately it rarely bites people. It is found in tropical rain
forests from Sierra Leone on the West African coast east to
Sudan and south to Angola.

8

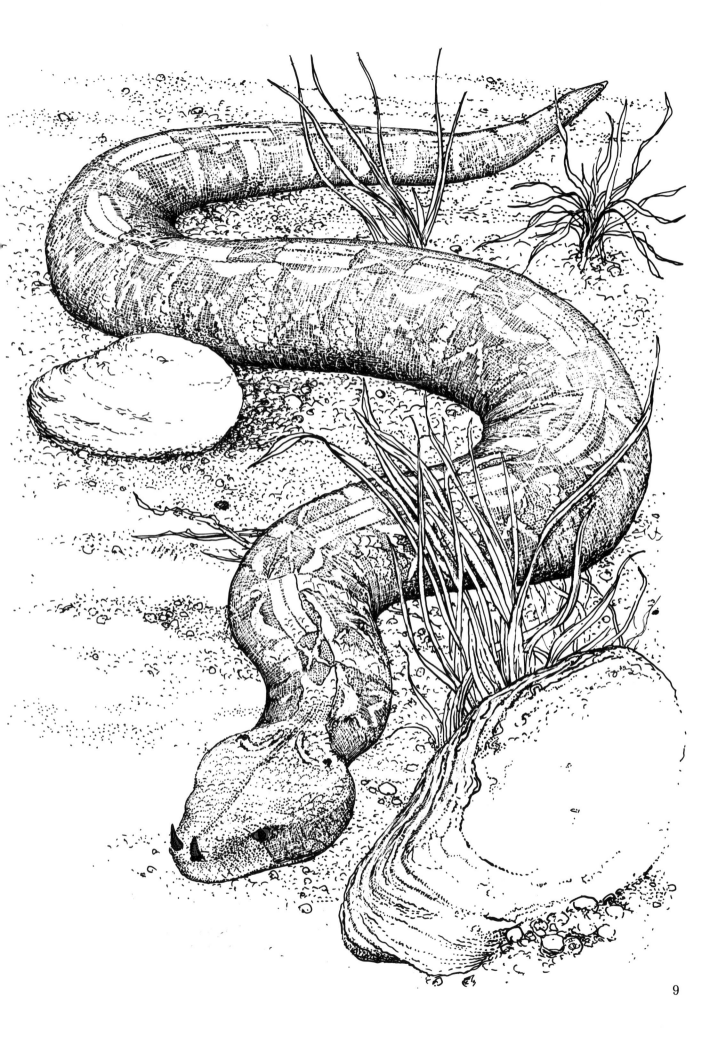

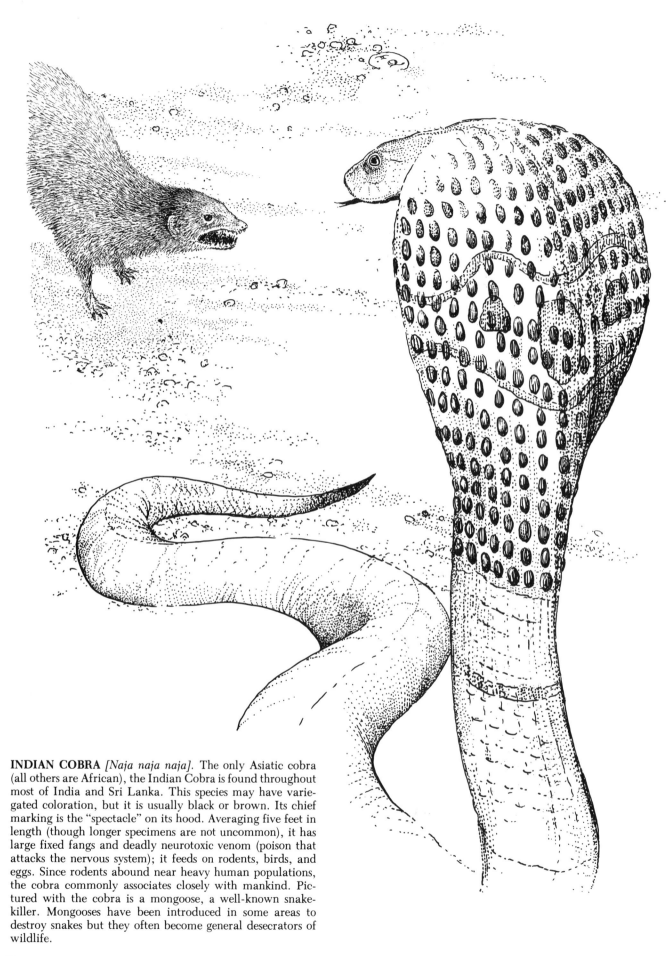

INDIAN COBRA *[Naja naja naja]*. The only Asiatic cobra (all others are African), the Indian Cobra is found throughout most of India and Sri Lanka. This species may have variegated coloration, but it is usually black or brown. Its chief marking is the "spectacle" on its hood. Averaging five feet in length (though longer specimens are not uncommon), it has large fixed fangs and deadly neurotoxic venom (poison that attacks the nervous system); it feeds on rodents, birds, and eggs. Since rodents abound near heavy human populations, the cobra commonly associates closely with mankind. Pictured with the cobra is a mongoose, a well-known snake-killer. Mongooses have been introduced in some areas to destroy snakes but they often become general desecrators of wildlife.

LEOPARD LIZARD *[Crotaphytus wistizenii]* (TOP). A gray to brownish lizard about five inches long with spots reminiscent of a leopard's, it has conspicuous crossbars on body and tail. Like a chameleon, it can change color. This fast lizard, which ranges from Oregon and Idaho south into Mexico, uses its hind legs only when running at top speed. Similar to the Leopard Lizard in having crossbars on its body and spots on the body and tail, the **COLLARED LIZARD** *[Crotaphytus collaris]* (BOTTOM) is 4½ inches long, with a conspicuous black-and-white collar and a head larger than that of the Leopard Lizard. Its ground color varies from green and blue to brown and yellow. It lives among mountain rocks and gullies from Oregon and Idaho east to Missouri and south into Mexico.

Frequently and incorrectly called "horned toads," horned lizards, including the **PACIFIC** or **COAST HORNED LIZARD** *[Phrynosoma coronatum]* (TOP), are covered with scales, and are thus reptiles, not amphibians. Alleged to shoot blood from their eyes, horned lizards are four inches long and have variable coloration that matches their environment. Resembling miniature dinosaurs, they have long "horns" at the back of the head and fringe-scales along their sides. They prefer sandy soil but are also found in washes, brushlands, and forests in the western U.S. The **CHUCKWALLA** *[Sauromalus obesus]* (BOTTOM) looks obese because of the many folds of loose skin on its neck and sides. This colorful sun-lover of the southwestern U.S. grows to about fourteen inches and has a blunt, broad-based tail. Most lizards are insectivorous, but the Chuckwalla is herbivorous, eating primarily the creosote

bush; this diet results in long, cylindrical feces that lead directly to its haunt. It will retreat when approached, however, distending and wedging its body into a rocky crevice, making it difficult to remove.

The most common American lizard, found from southern Missouri to Pennsylvania, the **FENCE** or **PINE LIZARD** *[Sceloporus undulatus]* (OPPOSITE), hopes, when approached, that its camouflage will protect it as it scurries to the far side of the pine tree or weathered fence rail where it is usually seen. Both sexes of this spiny creature have iridescent greenish-blue patches on top. The male (TOP) also has large patches that nearly meet in the middle of the belly and some color on the throat. The patches on the female (BOTTOM) are smaller. She also has dark, wavy lines across the back.

GILA MONSTER *[Heloderma suspectum].* The Gila (pronounced *hee'la*) Monster, one of the world's two venomous lizards (the other is *Heloderma horridum,* the **MEXICAN BEADED LIZARD** [not pictured]), can grow to 23 inches and weigh 3¼ pounds. Thick-bodied, with a thick head and tail, its color varies from the usual pink and black to yellowish or orangish and black. The tail is used for storage, providing energy during lean times or aestivation. The venom is produced in glands in the lower jaw and enters wounds through grooves in the teeth. Now an endangered species, it most frequently is found in arid or semiarid canyons and arroyos of Arizona, New Mexico, and Mexico.

14

The only truly marine lizard, the **MARINE IGUANA** *[Amblyrhynchus cristatus]* feeds on seaweed. It is endemic to the Galápagos Islands, where it may grow to three feet, the length varying from island to island. Usually all Marine Iguanas are considered to be a single species, but there are obvious differences among specimens, leading some authorities to dis-

tinguish seven forms. Some specimens are black; the most colorful are those on Hood Island, which are brilliant orange, mottled red, and black, with green forelegs and a green crest extending from head to tail. The Marine Iguana drinks sea water, ejecting excess salt through a pair of glands near its nostrils.

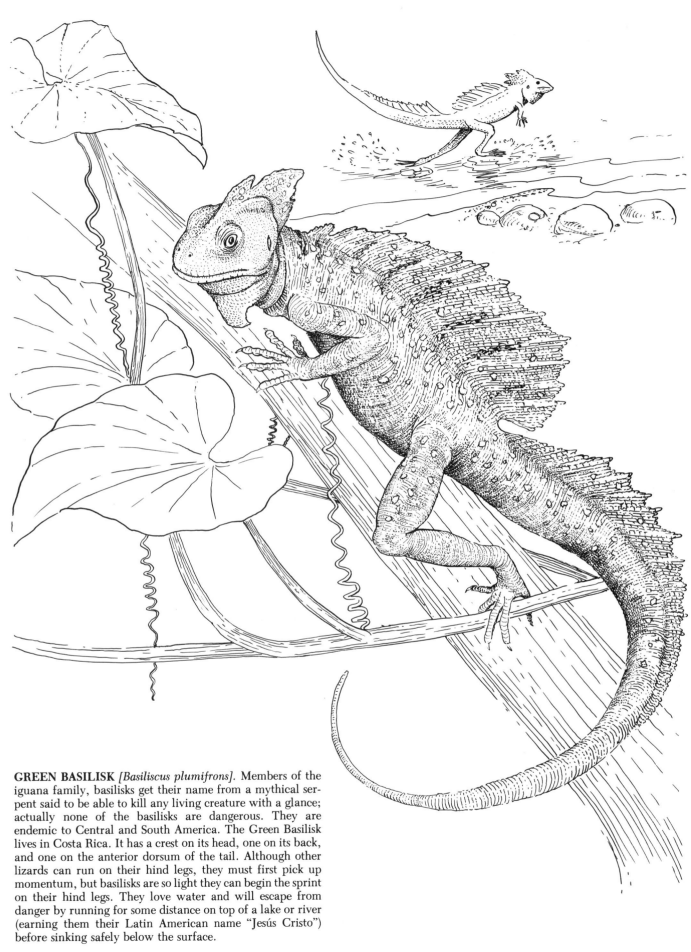

GREEN BASILISK *[Basiliscus plumifrons].* Members of the iguana family, basilisks get their name from a mythical serpent said to be able to kill any living creature with a glance; actually none of the basilisks are dangerous. They are endemic to Central and South America. The Green Basilisk lives in Costa Rica. It has a crest on its head, one on its back, and one on the anterior dorsum of the tail. Although other lizards can run on their hind legs, they must first pick up momentum, but basilisks are so light they can begin the sprint on their hind legs. They love water and will escape from danger by running for some distance on top of a lake or river (earning them their Latin American name "Jesús Cristo") before sinking safely below the surface.

16

THORNY DEVIL *[Moloch horridus]*. Take a handful of sharp, prickly thorns with red, brown, gray, aqua, yellow, orange, and white paint splashed over them; stir; and shape like a lizard: now you have one of the most bizarre small lizards in the world, *Moloch horridus*, named after the legendary Canaanite god to whom children were sacrificed. This unbelievable creature lives in the arid areas of central Australia. It is an exaggerated **HORNED LIZARD** *[Phrynosoma]* (see page 12), with a similar diet. The Thorny Devil eats ants, but only those of a particular size. It can drink by absorbing water through its skin.

GREEN GECKO *[Phelsuma madagascariensis]* (OPPOSITE).
Geckoes today are tropicopolitan (that is, they inhabit all tropical regions). They differ in several ways from most other lizards, the Green Gecko even more than other geckoes because it is brightly colored and diurnal. It has a vividly green body with bright red lines running from eyes to nostrils and a number of bright red markings on the caudal or posterior half of the back. The toes are mostly light tan. Lizards usually have eyelids, but geckoes, like snakes, have a brille, a transparent scale covering the eye. The eyes have vertical pupils. Geckoes have small granular scales on their bodies and toes with friction pads that permit them to cling to and climb even glass panes and to walk across ceilings. The Green Gecko is found in Madagascar.

FRILLED LIZARD *[Chlamydosaurus kingii]*. An Australian lizard that frequently runs swiftly on its hind legs using its tail for balance, much as a kangaroo uses its tail when leaping along at great speeds. Folds of skin on the sides of the neck may be quickly opened like an umbrella in order to intimidate an enemy or to make it difficult for the Frilled Lizard to be swallowed. Fully expanded, the blue, scarlet, and yellow frill may be over eight inches across; the entire lizard, tail included, is about three feet long. To appear more ferocious, the lizard holds its mouth open and stands tall on its front legs.

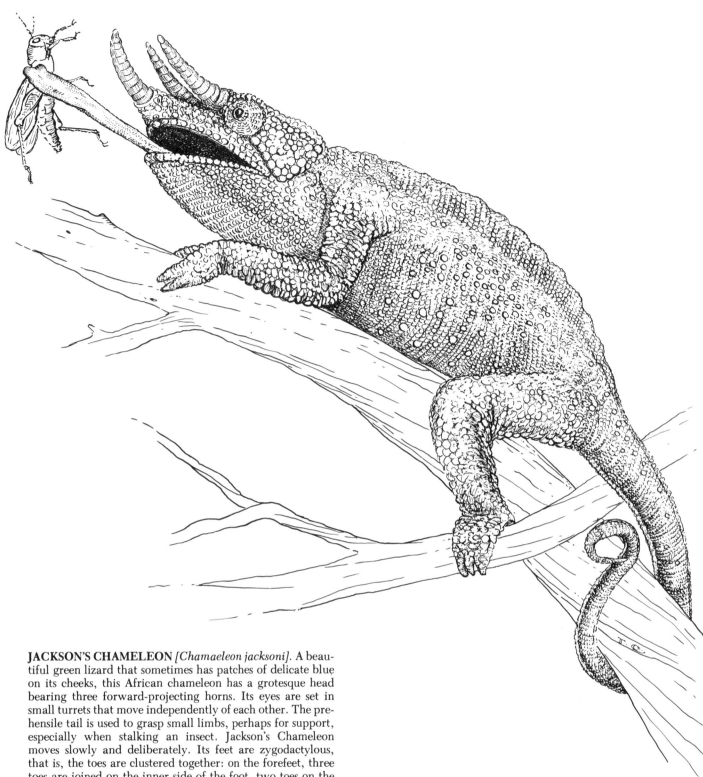

JACKSON'S CHAMELEON *[Chamaeleon jacksoni].* A beautiful green lizard that sometimes has patches of delicate blue on its cheeks, this African chameleon has a grotesque head bearing three forward-projecting horns. Its eyes are set in small turrets that move independently of each other. The prehensile tail is used to grasp small limbs, perhaps for support, especially when stalking an insect. Jackson's Chameleon moves slowly and deliberately. Its feet are zygodactylous, that is, the toes are clustered together: on the forefeet, three toes are joined on the inner side of the foot, two toes on the outer side; the hind feet have the reverse arrangement. The tongue, folded like an accordion in the mouth, can reach out to a length equal to that of the entire animal (that is, on the average about 6 inches). Colors can change to pale yellow and brown or to a mottled pattern.

Once an important source of food, the **WOOD TURTLE** *[Clemmys insculpta]* (OPPOSITE, TOP) grows to about eight inches, and has an orange neck and legs and a very rough shell with each scute or carapace plate rising to a peak of concentric ridges. Pollution, habitat destruction, overcollecting, and highway fatalities have greatly reduced its numbers. It is most common in northeastern U.S. to Nova Scotia. Although there is much disagreement among scientists about terminology, some would argue that, strictly speaking, the **DIAMONDBACK TERRAPIN** *[Malaclemys terrapin]* (OPPOSITE, BOTTOM) is the world's only terrapin; turtle, terrapins, and tortoises are different offshoots of the same limb (order Testudinata) of the evolutionary tree. Found along the coast from Cape Cod to Cape Hatteras in salt marshes and brackish waters, it is the chief ingredient of the gourmet's "Terrapin à la Maryland." Nearly nine inches long with variable coloration, it usually has a shell pattern of dark rings on a light ground, and the head and legs are generously spotted.

How can you tell a turtle from a tortoise? The terminology differs around the world; in the U.S. we say "tortoise" for a land animal, "turtle" for an aquatic or semiaquatic animal. There are two main types of **GALÁPAGOS TORTOISE** *[Geochelone elephantopus]*, an animal endemic to the Galápagos (or Tortoise) Islands: one has a dome-shaped upper shell, one a saddle-shaped shell. There are 15 subspecies; 10 are found on separate islands; five are found on Isabella Island, which once consisted of several islands until volcanic eruptions joined them. The Galápagos Tortoise has elephantine legs to support weights that may exceed 400 pounds. These tortoises play a special role in the history of biology, for it was in part while contemplating them and the birds we now know as Darwin's Finches that Charles Darwin developed his theory of natural selection. Darwin concluded that all life is locked in a struggle to survive, but only those individuals properly adapted to a changing environment will do so.

One aspect of a changing environment is the influence of man. The Galápagos Tortoises were used as a source of food by ships' crews from the seventeenth to the nineteenth century. Thus these marvelous animals have become extinct on many islands.

The **MUSK TURTLE** *[Sternotherus odoratus]* (TOP), known commonly as the **STINKPOT TURTLE,** is found in muddy, reedy ponds or clear bodies of water, including lakes throughout most of the eastern U.S. Frequently caught on hook and line when it steals the bait meant for a fish, it grows to about 4½ inches and is readily identified by two distinct light stripes on its head. The notorious **SNAPPING TURTLE** *[Chelydra serpentina]* (BOTTOM) is a source of delicious meat. Its shell may reach 18 inches. A long, agile neck and a head with a powerful, sharp beak, accompanied by a terrible disposition, make the "snapper" dangerous. It eats both useful and junk fish, young waterfowl, and such mammals as the muskrat. Colored from black to brown and often covered by algae, this turtle is difficult to see in its preferred murky waters. It is common in the entire eastern U.S.

24

BOG or MUHLENBERG'S TURTLE [*Clemmys muhlenbergii*] (TOP). Handsome and much sought after, the Bog Turtle was once common, but habitat destruction (not collecting) has made it rare. Several states, including New York, New Jersey, and Pennsylvania, grant it legal protection, which means that there are heavy fines for possessing or destroying this turtle. The Bog Turtle also is found in North Carolina, Maryland, and Virginia. About 3½ inches long and frequenting clear meadow streams and bogs, it has a dark shell and head with a bright orange spot on either side of the back of the head and neck. More common and widely distributed is the EASTERN PAINTED TURTLE [*Chrysemys p. picta*] (BELOW), also known as the POND TURTLE or PAINTED TERRAPIN. Found on the Atlantic coastal plain, it grows to about six inches and is dark green with red marks on the marginal scutes of the upper shell. Attractive green and yellow stripes appear on the head. The lower shell is yellow and the underside of the marginal scutes of the upper shell may be vivid red, yellow, and green.

BLANDING'S TURTLE [*Emydoidea blandingi*] (TOP). An aquatic turtle commonly found on land in the Great Lakes region of the U.S., it grows to about eight inches. It may have yellow spots or streaks, but its distinguishing trait is a bright yellow area under the lower jaw and neck. A turtle that is really terrestrial but enjoys soaking in puddles and mud, the **EASTERN BOX TURTLE** [*Terrapene c. carolina*] (MIDDLE) is a common pet in the Midwest and the eastern U.S. It grows to six inches and has a high upper shell. Its color varies but is generally yellow or orange on black. Males' eyes are red to pink, females' are yellowish. The slightly smaller **ORNATE BOX TURTLE** [*Terrapene o. ornata*] (BOTTOM) ranges in the plains states of the central U.S. Three sets of yellow lines directed downward and other yellow lines higher on the upper shell make identification easy. Unfortunately hundreds of these turtles are killed every year on highways where they bask in the sun.

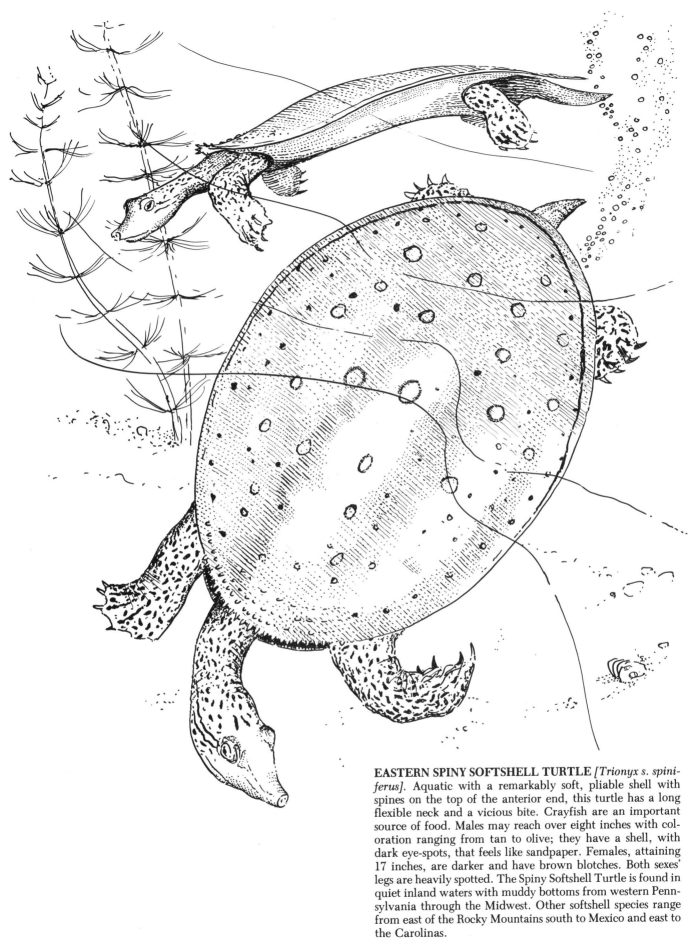

EASTERN SPINY SOFTSHELL TURTLE *[Trionyx s. spiniferus]*. Aquatic with a remarkably soft, pliable shell with spines on the top of the anterior end, this turtle has a long flexible neck and a vicious bite. Crayfish are an important source of food. Males may reach over eight inches with coloration ranging from tan to olive; they have a shell, with dark eye-spots, that feels like sandpaper. Females, attaining 17 inches, are darker and have brown blotches. Both sexes' legs are heavily spotted. The Spiny Softshell Turtle is found in quiet inland waters with muddy bottoms from western Pennsylvania through the Midwest. Other softshell species range from east of the Rocky Mountains south to Mexico and east to the Carolinas.

27

MATAMATA TURTLE *[Chelus fimbriatus]*. The weird Matamata, endemic to the northeastern tropical waters of South America, is a formidable predator that is almost impossible to see because of its camouflage of greenish-brown neck and leg skin and a ridged shell covered with green algae. At the end of its long neck and strange head with wavy folds of skin is its suction-pump mouth which draws fish into it to be swallowed. Unlike most turtles, it does not have a horny-beaked mouth; the suction action and quick swallowing eliminate the need for biting or chewing. A long, protracted nose allows it to breathe while its entire body is underwater.

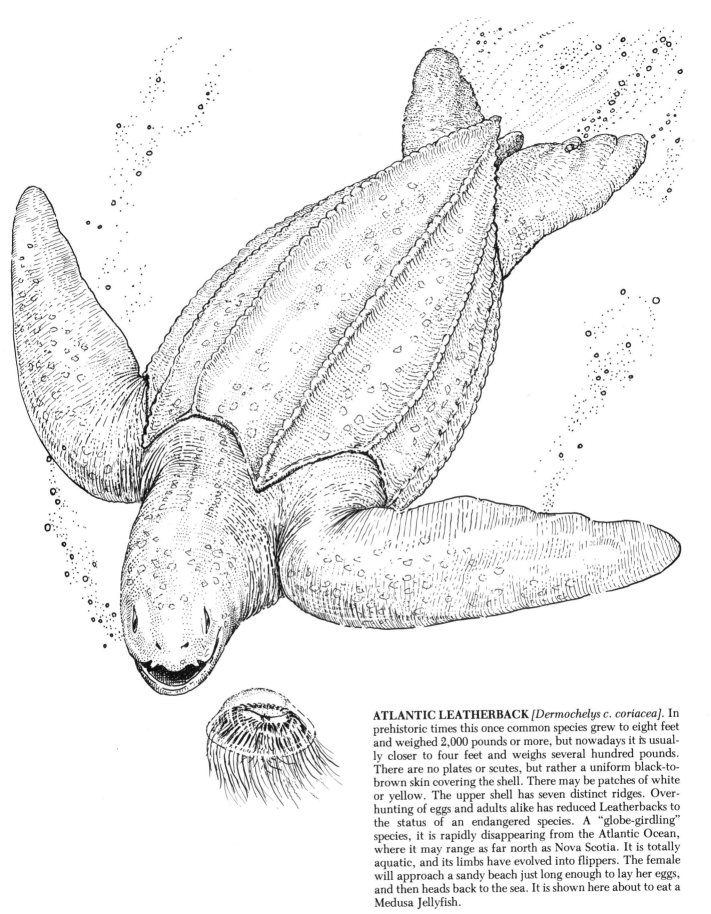

ATLANTIC LEATHERBACK *[Dermochelys c. coriacea].* In prehistoric times this once common species grew to eight feet and weighed 2,000 pounds or more, but nowadays it is usually closer to four feet and weighs several hundred pounds. There are no plates or scutes, but rather a uniform black-to-brown skin covering the shell. There may be patches of white or yellow. The upper shell has seven distinct ridges. Over-hunting of eggs and adults alike has reduced Leatherbacks to the status of an endangered species. A "globe-girdling" species, it is rapidly disappearing from the Atlantic Ocean, where it may range as far north as Nova Scotia. It is totally aquatic, and its limbs have evolved into flippers. The female will approach a sandy beach just long enough to lay her eggs, and then heads back to the sea. It is shown here about to eat a Medusa Jellyfish.

29

DUSKY SALAMANDER *[Desmognathus f. fuscus]* (OPPO-SITE, TOP). *Dusky* is the best word to describe any of the many varieties of this inconspicuous, grayish-to-brown species of amphibian. From 2½ to four inches long, Duskies live in wet areas along streams and springs from Maine to Louisiana. The female may curl around a few eggs beneath a rock or log. The common, slender **NORTHERN TWO-LINED SALA-MANDER** *[Eurycea b. bislineata]* (OPPOSITE, BOTTOM) is found under flat stones along the edge of deeper areas of small streams or under stones in shallow water. Yellow with two dark lateral lines and a row of darker spots over the back-bone, it reaches from 2½ to 3½ inches. Ranges throughout eastern and midwestern U.S. except most of Florida.

BARRED TIGER SALAMANDER *[Ambystoma tigrinum mavortium]* (TOP). An attractive salamander running to eight inches in length, it often remains neotenic, that is, it keeps larval characteristics even when sexually mature. The black-ish ground color is brightly marked with yellow bars on the sides and a yellow midline down the back. It is found from Nebraska to northern Mexico. The **EASTERN TIGER SALA-MANDER** *[Ambystoma t. tigrinum]* (BOTTOM) is similar in size and color to the Barred Tiger Salamander, but it is found throughout most of the eastern U.S., except New England, and in the Appalachian region. Its light spots are often green-ish yellow or yellowish brown; sometime there is no yellow at all. The spots are irregularly shaped and distributed.

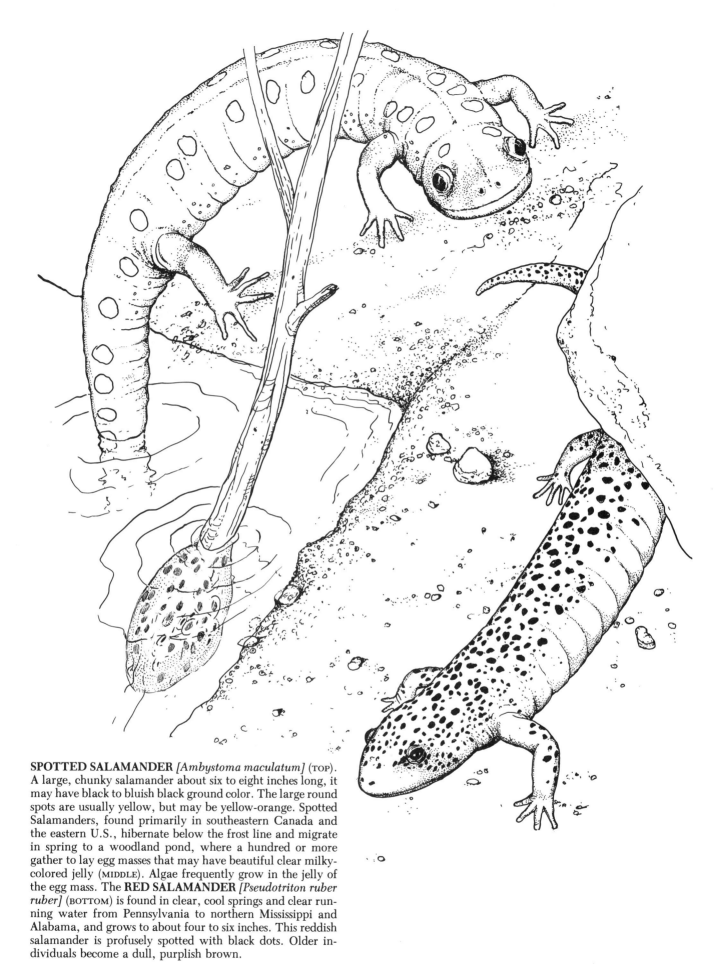

SPOTTED SALAMANDER *[Ambystoma maculatum]* (TOP). A large, chunky salamander about six to eight inches long, it may have black to bluish black ground color. The large round spots are usually yellow, but may be yellow-orange. Spotted Salamanders, found primarily in southeastern Canada and the eastern U.S., hibernate below the frost line and migrate in spring to a woodland pond, where a hundred or more gather to lay egg masses that may have beautiful clear milky-colored jelly (MIDDLE). Algae frequently grow in the jelly of the egg mass. The **RED SALAMANDER** *[Pseudotriton ruber ruber]* (BOTTOM) is found in clear, cool springs and clear running water from Pennsylvania to northern Mississippi and Alabama, and grows to about four to six inches. This reddish salamander is profusely spotted with black dots. Older individuals become a dull, purplish brown.

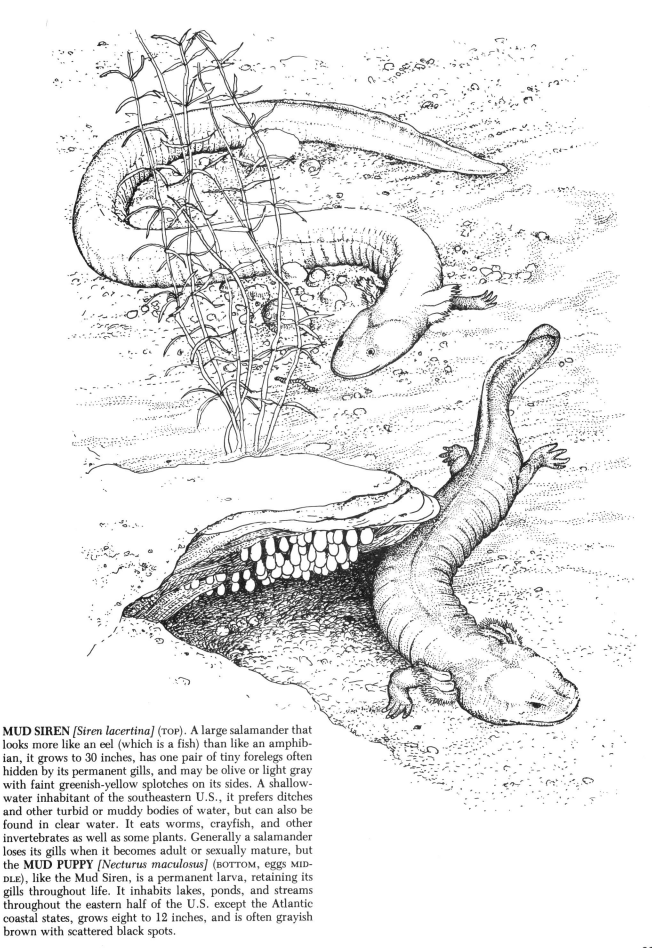

MUD SIREN *[Siren lacertina]* (TOP). A large salamander that looks more like an eel (which is a fish) than like an amphibian, it grows to 30 inches, has one pair of tiny forelegs often hidden by its permanent gills, and may be olive or light gray with faint greenish-yellow splotches on its sides. A shallow-water inhabitant of the southeastern U.S., it prefers ditches and other turbid or muddy bodies of water, but can also be found in clear water. It eats worms, crayfish, and other invertebrates as well as some plants. Generally a salamander loses its gills when it becomes adult or sexually mature, but the **MUD PUPPY** *[Necturus maculosus]* (BOTTOM, eggs MIDDLE), like the Mud Siren, is a permanent larva, retaining its gills throughout life. It inhabits lakes, ponds, and streams throughout the eastern half of the U.S. except the Atlantic coastal states, grows eight to 12 inches, and is often grayish brown with scattered black spots.

TEXAS BLIND SALAMANDER *[Typhlomolge rathbuni].* Appearing more like a creature from Mars than an earthly salamander, this is a white, blind species about four inches in length, one of several species of similar salamanders living in the waters of limestone subterranean regions in the southern U.S. This species is easily identified by its shovel-like nose and long, spindly legs. Eyes and pigment are absent and unnecessary, since these amphibians live in total darkness. Such species are seen only when caves are explored or when, on rare occasions, they are pumped out of artesian wells. The blind salamanders are neotenic, that is, they retain their gills throughout life.

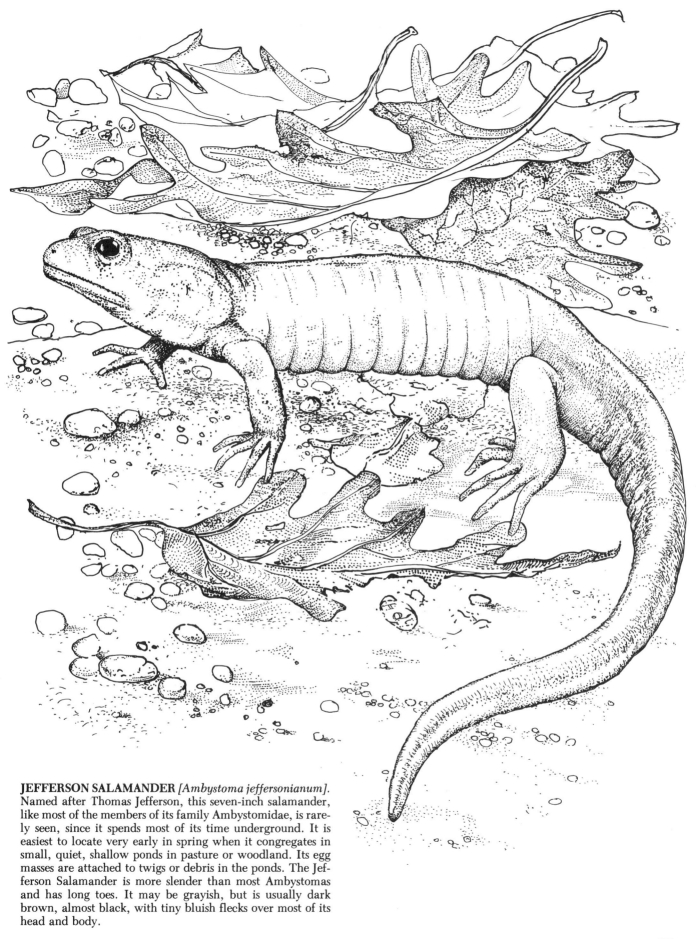

JEFFERSON SALAMANDER *[Ambystoma jeffersonianum]*.
Named after Thomas Jefferson, this seven-inch salamander,
like most of the members of its family Ambystomidae, is rarely seen, since it spends most of its time underground. It is
easiest to locate very early in spring when it congregates in
small, quiet, shallow ponds in pasture or woodland. Its egg
masses are attached to twigs or debris in the ponds. The Jefferson Salamander is more slender than most Ambystomas
and has long toes. It may be grayish, but is usually dark
brown, almost black, with tiny bluish flecks over most of its
head and body.

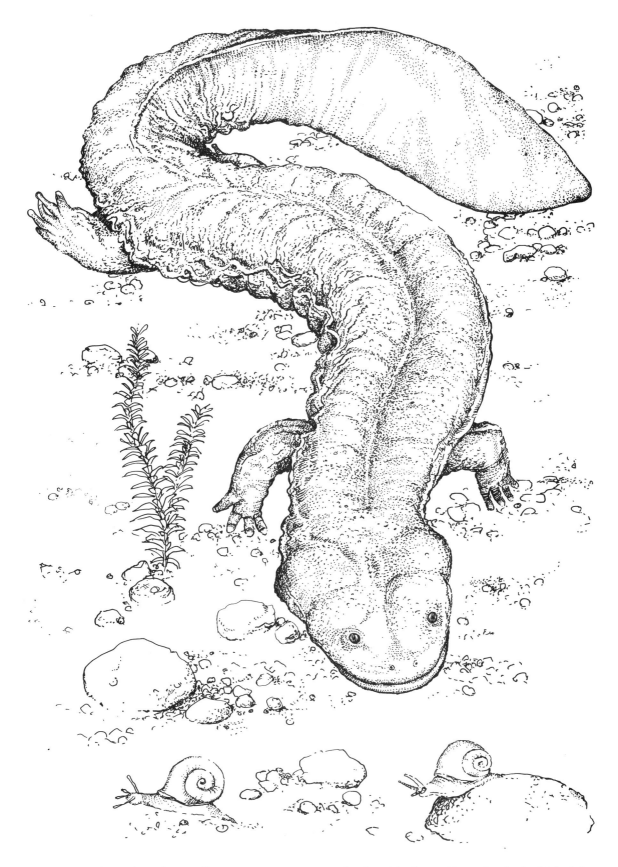

HELLBENDER [*Cryptobranchus a. alleganiensis*] counts as the largest American salamander when mass, length, and width are all taken into consideration; only the much slenderer Sirens are longer. It is usually 10 to 20 inches long, but some specimens are nearly 30 inches (its Japanese relative, *Megalobatrachus japonicus*, reaches five feet). Completely aquatic, the Hellbender loses its gills in adulthood. Its grayish head and body are flat and a fleshy fold of skin runs along each side of the body. Commonly and fallaciously thought to be poisonous (it even looks dangerous), it is perfectly innocuous. It is found in clear, fairly deep streams and rivers draining the Appalachian Mountains from southern Pennsylvania to northern Alabama.

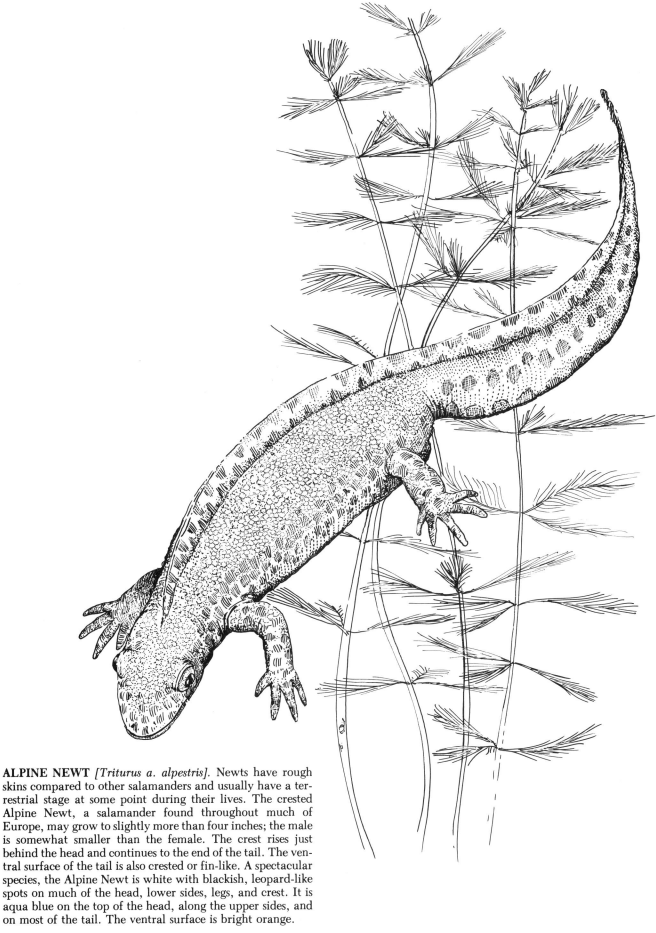

ALPINE NEWT *[Triturus a. alpestris]*. Newts have rough
skins compared to other salamanders and usually have a terrestrial stage at some point during their lives. The crested
Alpine Newt, a salamander found throughout much of
Europe, may grow to slightly more than four inches; the male
is somewhat smaller than the female. The crest rises just
behind the head and continues to the end of the tail. The ventral surface of the tail is also crested or fin-like. A spectacular
species, the Alpine Newt is white with blackish, leopard-like
spots on much of the head, lower sides, legs, and crest. It is
aqua blue on the top of the head, along the upper sides, and
on most of the tail. The ventral surface is bright orange.

Frogs are smooth-skinned, web-footed, largely aquatic, tail-less amphibians. The **STRAWBERRY FROG** *[Dendrobates pumilio]* is a gorgeous frog about one inch long. The common name is derived from the strawberry-red color of the body, which is sprinkled with small black dots. The forefeet and hind legs are brownish black to black. These frogs are found in jungle foliage, but are not true tree dwellers, as the genus name *Dendrobates* would imply; rather they live in the jungle's lower story. All of the members of *Dendrobates* inhabit the New World tropics and are known as the **ARROW POISON FROGS.** Indians extract poison from the skin and dip their arrows in it. Such an arrow can paralyze a small animal instantly.

WOOD FROG *[Rana sylvatica]* (TOP). The "Lone Ranger" of the frog world wears a dark mask from behind the eyes to the shoulders. Nearly three inches long, it can change its color from delicate pink to chocolate brown. It breeds in ponds in a few days in very early spring, and then returns to the woods. It has the northernmost range of any American frog: from Alaska to Labrador and, in the east, south to northern Georgia. The **PICKEREL FROG** *[Rana palustris]* (MIDDLE) is excellent bait for pickerel fishing, even though its poison glands — with poison strong enough to kill other frogs kept together with it in a small container — make it unpalatable for most frog-eating predators. Square to rectangular dark markings on a usually tan ground conceal bright yellow-orange

groins. It has a low-pitched snore and frequents cool water in southeastern Canada and the eastern half of the U.S. The **LEOPARD** or **MEADOW FROG** *[Rana p. pipiens]* (BOTTOM) varies considerably in color, but is usually brown or green with light-bordered spots. The undersurface, groins included, is pure white. Its distinctive heavy snore may be heard near ponds throughout most of southern Canada, all but the westernmost part of the U.S., and well into Mexico.

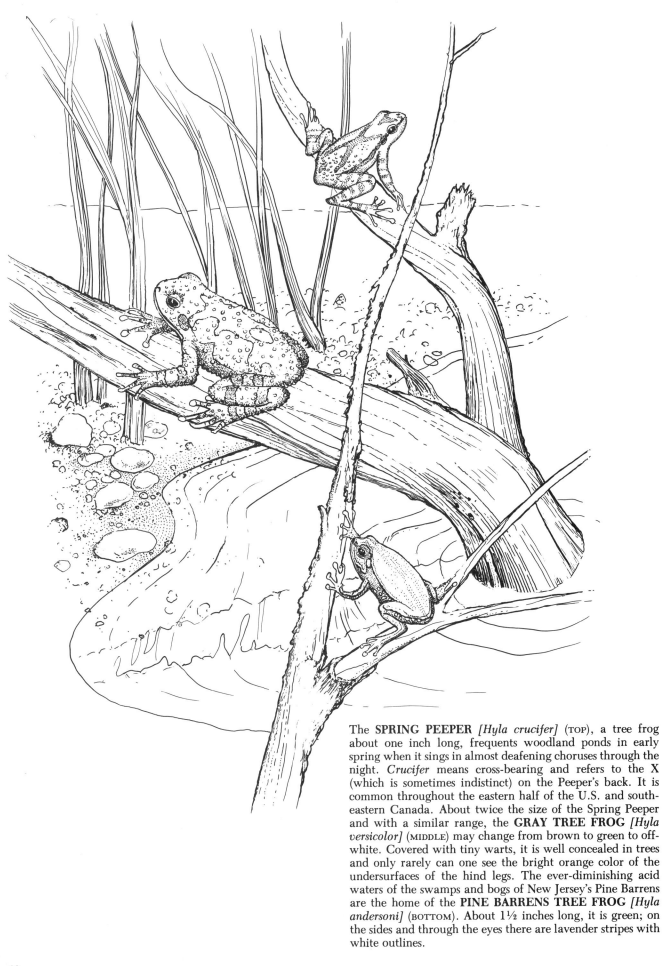

The **SPRING PEEPER** *[Hyla crucifer]* (TOP), a tree frog about one inch long, frequents woodland ponds in early spring when it sings in almost deafening choruses through the night. *Crucifer* means cross-bearing and refers to the X (which is sometimes indistinct) on the Peeper's back. It is common throughout the eastern half of the U.S. and southeastern Canada. About twice the size of the Spring Peeper and with a similar range, the **GRAY TREE FROG** *[Hyla versicolor]* (MIDDLE) may change from brown to green to offwhite. Covered with tiny warts, it is well concealed in trees and only rarely can one see the bright orange color of the undersurfaces of the hind legs. The ever-diminishing acid waters of the swamps and bogs of New Jersey's Pine Barrens are the home of the **PINE BARRENS TREE FROG** *[Hyla andersoni]* (BOTTOM). About 1½ inches long, it is green; on the sides and through the eyes there are lavender stripes with white outlines.

Similar to the Spring Peeper, the **MOUNTAIN CHORUS FROG** [*Pseudacris brachyphona*] (TOP LEFT) is light tan with two curved darker brown lines on the back that almost resemble an X. There is a small brownish triangle between the eyes. It is found at high altitudes, to almost 4,000 feet, from southwestern Pennsylvania to Alabama. Classed with the tree frogs even though it does not climb, the **NORTHERN CRICKET FROG** [*Acris c. crepitans*] (TOP RIGHT) is about one inch long with greatly varying colors and patterns; usually it is greenish with brownish legs and body stripes. Its range is from New Jersey to eastern Texas. The **BOREAL CHORUS FROG** [*Pseudacris triseriata maculata*] (MIDDLE) is the northernmost chorus frog (as *Boreal* implies). Brownish and greenish with

three stripes, which are sometimes indistinct, it ranges in Canada and the U.S. from the Rockies to the Midwest. Brownish or grayish, the patterns of the **UPLAND CHORUS FROG** [*Pseudacris triseriata feriarum*] (BOTTOM LEFT) are extremely varied; the most distinctive mark is a dark stripe from eye to groin. Habitats include bogs, ponds, marshes, moist woodlands, and grasslands from eastern Pennsylvania to Texas. Like a chameleon, the **ORNATE CHORUS FROG** [*Pseudacris ornata*] (BOTTOM RIGHT) can change colors. There are dark spots on the back and sides (hence *ornata*) of this beautiful small frog, which is found from North Carolina to Louisiana.

41

Often and irrelevantly referred to as the **RAIN FROG**, the **GREEN TREE FROG** *[Hyla cinerea]* (LEFT) is strikingly beautiful in its vivid green coat with yellowish side stripes. Barely two inches long, Green Frogs are very common along lakes and streams and in swamps. During mating season the males fill the air with their bell-like voices. This frog is found from Washington, D.C., to eastern Texas, but is most common in the southeastern U.S. The **BARKING TREE FROG** *[Hyla gratiosa]* (RIGHT) grows to about two inches or slightly more and can be heard "barking" from the heights of trees. Mostly green with dark spots generously distributed on its back, this species, like a chameleon, can change its color. It is a coastal-plain frog found from North Carolina to eastern Louisiana.

BULLFROG [*Rana catesbeiana*]. This is the largest American frog, growing up to eight inches. Its hind legs are highly valued as a delicacy. Smaller Bulfrogs closely resemble the **GREEN FROG** [*Rana clamitans*] (not pictured), but the Bullfrog's dorso-lateral line partly encircles and ends at the eardrum or tympanum, whereas for *R. clamitans* the line runs to the hip. The Bullfrog varies considerably, especially from region to region, in color and pattern. Tadpoles may take as long as two years to mature; for other frog species tadpoles may mature in a few weeks or a year. The Bullfrog prefers large bodies of water and occurs naturally in the eastern two-thirds of the U.S.; its range has been artificially extended to California and Mexico.

ZATEK'S FROG *[Atelopus zeteki]* (OPPOSITE, TOP); **GOLDEN FROG** *[Atelopus varius zeteki]* (OPPOSITE, BOTTOM). A genus of colorful frogs, *Atelopus* is found throughout much of Central and South America. The two species illustrated here are bright gold. Zatek's Frog is usually characterized by the presence of black spots or patches. The Golden Frog may have black markings or, under certain conditions, as when sitting in bright sunlight, may appear to have no markings at all. Both species are inactive at night and are members of the poison-frog group. To be effective, however, their deadly poison must enter a cut or mucous membrane and into the bloodstream. Thus these frogs may be handled freely as long as one does not have any open cuts on the hands.

Toads are easily distinguished from frogs: their backs are flatter, their legs shorter, their skin dull and wrinkled; they lay their eggs in strings instead of in masses; and they hop or walk instead of leaping. The **AMERICAN TOAD** *[Bufo americanus]* (TOP), also known as the **HOPTOAD**, is similar to **FOWLER'S TOAD** *[Bufo woodhousei fowleri]* (LEFT), except that the American Toad has one or two warts in each of its many dark spots and the large parotid glands on the back of the head are usually separated from the ridge behind the eye; Fowler's Toad has three or more warts to the dark spots and the parotid glands usually touch the ridge behind the eye. Both toads exceed three inches, vary greatly in color, and range throughout most of the eastern U.S., but are especially common along the Atlantic coastal plain. The **SPADEFOOT TOAD** *[Scaphiopus holbrooki]* (RIGHT) has a sharp "spade" on the hind foot that enables it to dig easily in loose, generally sandy soil. It ranges sporadically east of the Mississippi.

INDEX